The First
EASTER

The First Easter

Written and illustrated by Carol Heyer

ideals children's books.

Nashville, Tennessee

ISBN-13: 978-0-8249-5576-2

Published by Ideals Children's Books
An imprint of Ideals Publications
A Guideposts Company
535 Metroplex Drive, Suite 250
Nashville, Tennessee 37211
www.idealsbooks.com

Color separations by Precision Color Graphics, Franklin, Wisconsin
Printed and bound in Italy by LEGO

Library of Congress CIP data on file

The illustrations in this book were rendered in acrylic paints and use
live models.

*Special thanks to Chase Philip Atkinson, Skylar Rae Atkinson,
David Atkinson, Suzan Davis Atkinson, Chanel Ray, Miles Ray,
Daniel Singh, and Darci Ann Evans.*

10 9 8 7 6 5 4 3 2

To my parents, Merlyn and Bill Heyer, as a
small acknowledgment of their boundless love
and support; and for my sister, Suzan.
—C.H.

 # At Eastertime

we think of fresh new grass and baby animals and warm,
golden sunshine. We think of baskets full of candy and
brilliantly colored eggs. But most of all, at Eastertime we
think about Jesus and all that he did for us.

Jesus was born in a manger in Bethlehem on the first Christmas Day. Angels told shepherds about the Babe, and they went to see the child.

A great star shone above the manger, and its sparkling light led the Magi to Baby Jesus. They came on camels and brought gifts; and they worshiped the newborn child, the Son of God.

Many years before Jesus' birth, prophets had foretold that God's Son would come to earth and save the world from sin.

When Jesus became a man, he chose twelve men to be his disciples. They traveled with Jesus, and he taught them about God.

Jesus healed the sick and crippled. Everywhere he went, many people gathered to hear him speak. Little children came to him also, and he greeted them with love and kindness.

When the time came for Jesus to fulfill the teachings of the prophets, he traveled to Jerusalem with his disciples. Jesus rode into the city on a donkey. People lined the streets to see him, and they laid palm branches on the ground to make a soft carpet for the donkey's feet. Jesus entered Jerusalem surrounded by love and glory on this, the first Palm Sunday.

Jesus went to the temple, where people worshiped. Inside, there were men buying and selling animals. Jesus was shocked and angry. He threw the money boxes into the air and the men ran away. This made the temple leaders very angry. They wanted to get rid of Jesus.

After the temple was clear, Jesus went inside to worship and to pray.

Inside the temple, Jesus talked about God's word with the chief priests and temple elders. They asked Jesus many questions and tried to trick him into saying something wrong.

The priests asked Jesus what was God's most important commandment.

Jesus answered, "Love God with all your heart." Then Jesus said, "But I give you a new commandment. You must love your neighbor as yourself."

The priests were very angry.

More and more people listened to Jesus as he taught about God. The temple leaders and priests grew more afraid of Jesus and began to plot against him. They looked for a way to have Jesus arrested.

On the night of the Feast of Unleavened Bread, Jesus and his disciples gathered together for the traditional Passover meal. Jesus broke his bread, gave thanks to God, then passed it to his disciples.

"This is my body which is given for you: this do in remembrance of me," he said.

Jesus then passed around the cup saying, "This is my blood which is shed for you."

This was the last time Jesus would eat with his disciples, and he wanted them to remember him in the future by sharing the bread and the cup. This was Jesus' last supper.

After supper, Jesus and his disciples went to the Garden of Gethsemane. Jesus went off to pray. When he returned, his disciples had fallen asleep.

Suddenly, soldiers came to the garden. They carried torches and spears. The soldiers arrested Jesus. The disciples wanted to fight, but Jesus said, "Do not fight. God's will be done."

The soldiers took Jesus to the court of Caiaphas, the high priest, where all the chief priests and elders had gathered. Caiaphas asked Jesus, "Are you Christ, the Son of God?"

Jesus replied, "Yes, it is as you say." Caiaphas said, "Take him to Pilate! He will judge him."

Each Passover, Pilate released one prisoner. He went out to the crowd and asked if he should release Jesus, but the people shouted for Jesus' death.

Soldiers led Jesus to the hill of Golgatha where they crucified him. Even though it was afternoon, the sky grew black, thunder roared, and lightning pierced the dark sky. At the moment of Jesus' death, a powerful earthquake shook the ground.

Before sunset, Jesus' friends took down his body and laid it in a tomb. A huge stone was rolled in front of the opening, and a soldier was sent to guard the tomb.

Early Sunday morning, three days after Jesus' death, his mother and two other women came to the tomb. They saw that the stone was rolled away; and when they entered the tomb, Jesus' body was gone. The women cried out, "Who took Jesus away?"

Suddenly, a man all in white appeared. "Why do you look for the living among the dead?" he asked. "Jesus is not here. He has risen!"

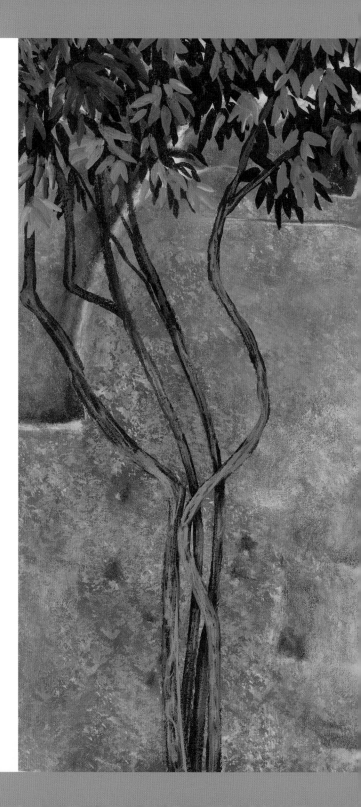

The women were so glad that they ran to tell the disciples Jesus was alive. When they heard the news, two disciples returned to the tomb with Mary Magdalene. They entered the tomb and found the burial clothes folded neatly. They left the tomb feeling afraid because Jesus was gone.

Mary Magdalene remained alone outside the tomb weeping. As she sobbed, she heard a man's voice ask her, "Why do you cry?"

Mary Magdalene replied, "Sir, if you have taken Jesus away, please tell me where you have put him."

The man whispered, "Mary."

Mary lifted her head and saw that it was Jesus who stood before her. She ran to tell the disciples that she had seen Jesus!

When Jesus appeared to his disciples, he said to them, "Go throughout the world. Tell the people what you have seen and heard. And I will be there with you always, even until the end of time."

This is why Christians celebrate Easter. We remember that Jesus gave up his life because he loved us. And on Easter morning, we rejoice because Jesus Christ rose from the dead. And we know that because of him, we, too, will live.